How to Embarrass Teachers

Poems chosen by

Paul Cookson

Illustrated by

David Parkins

MACMILLAN CHILDREN'S BOOKS

Dedicated to Steve Barlow and Steve Skidmore.
As The Two Steves they have probably embarrassed more
teachers than most writers put together.
Keep up the good work, lads!

First published 2006 by Macmillan Children's Books
a division of Macmillan Publishers Limited
20 New Wharf Road, London N1 9RR
Basingstoke and Oxford
www.panmacmillan.com

Associated companies throughout the world

ISBN-13: 978-0-330-44276-3
ISBN-10: 0-330-44276-7

A CIP catalogue record for this book is available from
the British Library.

Printed and bound in Great Britain by Mackays of Chatham plc, Kent

Contents

The Whoopee Cushion Waiting on the Teacher's Chair

All the class is silent
Our eyes are fixed on where
The whoopee cushion's waiting on our teacher's chair

First she paces to the right, then paces to the left
Carries on the lesson while perching on her desk
Nobody is moving, everybody stares
At the whoopee cushion waiting on our teacher's chair

We're praying for that moment, when she will sit down
Thinking of the giggling when we hear that funny sound
SQUEAK! BLART! HONK! FLURP! PARP! BLURRRR!
The whoopee cushion's waiting on our teacher's chair

It cannot be much longer now, we know that it will get 'er
The anticipated waiting will make it even better
Cos she hasn't got a clue, she hasn't got a care
That the whoopee cushion's waiting on our teacher's chair

What's that noise – creaking down the corridor
Our head teacher's coming – oh no! It's Mr Moore
We'd better all watch out, we'd better all beware
Cos the whoopee cushion's waiting on our teacher's chair

He's going to sit down on it! Oh no – disaster!
We're going to get in trouble now with our fat headmaster
It sounds like twenty tubas
Or a trumpet premiere
You should have seen him jump!
Ten feet in the air!
A red-faced ranting raver
He began to swear
Sounds that shook the ground
Vibrating everywhere
Sounds that bounced around
From behind his derrière
When the cushion was deflating on the teacher's chair

Everyone is frightened now, we're bound to get detention
But what happens next is beyond our comprehension
Mr Moor turns round to Miss and with an icy glare
He blames her for the whoopee cushion left upon the
    chair

Twice the embarrassment, twice the fun
Got two teachers for the price of one!
So much pleasure for us all to share . . .
Thanks to the whoopee cushion on the teacher's chair

Paul Cookson

Biting Mad

I love to make my teacher mad
I love to make him shout
Cos when his tongue gets tangled up
His new false teeth fall out.

Celia Gentles

Concise Hints for New Teachers

(Or . . . how not to be embarrassed in school)

1) If you get lost on your way to school,
   don't ask children for directions.
   (They may be dangerous.)

2) Think twice before wearing the jacket
   you imagined was trendy when you were
   a student.

3) Leave Teddy at home.
   (Yes, I know he misses you.)

4) On your first morning, don't confuse
   the head teacher with the caretaker.
   The caretaker will never forgive you.

5)   If someone shouts in the corridor,
      'Get into line and stop slouching,
      you scruffy article,'
      they are probably not shouting at you.

6)   It is right to enter the staffroom without
      knocking, and the staff toilet is no longer
      out of bounds.

7)   If you confiscate the *Beano* in class,
      don't be seen swapping it for bubblegum
      with the PE teacher.

8)   On open night, if one of the parents shouts
      at you, don't burst into tears.
      (Just make a note of the name
      and get your own back on the child later.)

9)   Practise scratching your nails down the blackboard
      – the kids will hate it.

10)   Bring sandwiches.

Roger McGough

Size

Boy!
Don't slouch
when you talk
to me.

Tom, age 10,
is 5 foot 9,
Mr Jones stands
5 foot 3.

I have to, Sir,
the boy replies,
for I cannot
hear you otherwise.

Jim Hatfield

Mrs Parsons

Mrs Parsons, my teacher, looks rather on edge.
I think it's because she knows
that I've brought some photographs into school.
Here's how the story goes:

She happens to live next door to us,
and her husband's name is Jack.
My brother kicked his football over her wall,
and her husband kicked it back.

I stuck my head over the wall to say thanks,
and who should be sat in a chair
on the lawn, but Mrs Parsons,
with curlers in her hair.

What's worse was her face was all covered in goo,
of a really hideous green.
She was wearing an old quilted dressing gown,
the dirtiest I've ever seen.

She screamed when she saw that I'd seen her
and disappeared quickly from view.
I'm so pleased I had my camera.
It's a digital one, and brand new!

Geraldine Aldridge

Silent Pee

Today in English
we did silent letters
The 'k' in knife
The 'b' in debtors
Teacher asked each of us
for an example
Brainbox Julian
gave her ample
When at last
she turned to me
I told her clearly
'Silent pee in sea'

Susan Bates

The Caretaker Leaves an Embarrassing Message on the Staffroom Noticeboard

'Dear Staff,

I've been to clean your toilets
With my germ-wipe and my broom
And I've found a pair of knickers
In the teachers' changing room.

They're in my cupboard, for you to collect . . .

(They're the largest size I've discovered yet!)'

Trevor Harvey

Kevin Confesses

Yes, it was me, Miss Jenkins,
I thought you'd be glad.
I'm sorry, Miss Jenkins,
the personal ad
I put in the paper
has turned out not good.
I'm sorry, Miss Jenkins,
I hoped that it would.

I'm sorry, Miss Jenkins,
that you're in a rage,
but how could I know
that isn't your age.
And I can see, Miss Jenkins,
how that got your goat,
cos you're fifteen years younger
than the number I wrote.

Yet well done, Miss Jenkins,
you've had four replies.
Not one you'd describe
though as 'happening guys'.
They've all got beer bellies,
one plays the drums,
one collects tractors,
two live with their mums.

I'm sorry, Miss Jenkins,
I can see you're upset
that I put 'can be blond
or attractive brunette'.
Don't cry now, Miss Jenkins,
you'll get yourself down –
your hair isn't 'mousy',
it's more 'interesting brown'.

I'm sorry, Miss Jenkins,
I won't do it again.
But can I just say
about my Uncle Len.
He's single, not ugly,
same interests as you,
'crosswords, fell walking'.
So would Uncle Len do?

He's an ace bloke, Miss Jenkins,
doesn't smoke, drink or bet.
He's a plumber, pays VAT,
with his own maisonette.
And if you got married
you'd stay at this school.
And I'd be your nephew!
Miss Jenkins – how cool!

Stewart Henderson

School Trip

It was soooo boring,
Until
Jenny had a nightmare.
Poor Jenny – but we got to see
Mr Tompkins in pink and yellow PJs
Ms Purvis in fluffy bunny slippers
and Mr Jones
in

     the biggest

     the reddest

     the silkiest

     the shiniest

     the longest

     the finest

nightshirt we'd ever seen.
And it all went quiet,
Until
Ms Purvis laughed.

Then Mr Tompkins laughed
then Jenny laughed
then we all laughed.
And Mr Jones
went so red
from his white-haired head
to his white-slippered feet
that he matched his nightshirt.

After that
it wasn't *quite* soooo boring.

Suzanne Elvidge

Oops!

When the teacher isn't looking
You should see the things we do –
Like putting tin tacks on their chairs
Or even superglue.

But once a trick backfired like mad –
For, once, before a test,
Somebody put some superglue
On Mr Thompson's desk.

As Thommo sat down on his chair
And looked up at the class
He put his elbow in the glue
And got himself stuck fast!

He yelled with rage and screamed like mad –
What was he to do?
Stuck there helpless like a moth
By a spot of superglue.

And then to make things even worse
We heard the fire alarm –
And there was Thommo, deathly white,
With a desk stuck on his arm!

Now fire alarms can be a prank,
Or maybe just a drill,
But sometimes they could be for real –
Old Thommo looked quite ill!

'Get me out, don't leave me here!'
He yelled in strangled voice,
So six of us picked up the desk –
I guess we'd got no choice.

So there we were, six kids, one desk,
One teacher, terrified,
His elbow still stuck fast with glue –
We took 'em both outside.

The fire engine screamed on in,
But it was just a bogus call –
The alarm had been a schoolboy prank,
A right mess all in all.

But the firemen were still needed,
Although not for any fire –
They had cut old Thommo free
As his temperature rose higher!

And as they got their axes out
To chop old Thommo free
I stood there thinking to myself,
'Best not to tell 'em it was me . . .'

Clive Webster

The Nappy Times

One of our most crafty school capers
followed a series in the local newspapers.
This was entitled 'All Our Yesterdays'
and featured old people, strange clothes and odd ways.
One photograph in particular was a real jewel –
so we kindly enlarged and copied it for the school.
At playtime we handed these out secretly, with care,
and, like fireworks, giggles exploded everywhere.
It displayed a certain happy little chappie
sporting an enormous white nappy.
It was, of course, our headmaster, having just won
the Bonniest Baby Competition of 1961!

Tim Pointon

Good Manners

'Good manners,' cried our teacher,
'good behaviour when you're out
are what I'd like to see
instead of layabouts and louts.
Considering your elders,
not getting into fights,
politeness to your teacher,
doing what is right.'
A shame we saw him shopping
with his tribe of squabbling sons,
who were running round him screaming,
having lots of fun.
Should we mention that he shouted
as they badgered him for toys
and a passing shopper muttered,
'Can't that man control those boys?'
No, we sat politely listening
as he droned away.
We'll save our little secret
for a rainy day.

Marian Swinger

The Inspector Calls

Hello, Mr Ofsted
Our teacher said you might
Choose someone to answer questions
And you've chosen me
I hope I get them right.

That's our teacher
In the playground on duty
She's usually in the staffroom
Drinking coffee
You can see the playground from there.

Do you like her pointy shoes
And smart black suit?
We're all making a special effort today
That's why I'm wearing uniform
Teacher usually wears an old tracksuit.

Do you like our golden carp?
He's called Henry the Eighth
The other seven died
Teacher's not very good with fish.
(Or hamsters, actually.)

Teacher's very organized.
Except of course that time
When she lost the register
And it turned up three days later
At Fat Freddy's Big Fried Takeaway.
Go figure!

Oh, and we had to say – she's very calm.
Actually she fell asleep once in literacy hour.
Still, like she says
There's more to life
Then knowing where to put a comma.

Mr Ofsted, I hope I was helpful
Teacher says that's what we're here for
So now you're my mate
Please don't hesitate
To come back if you want to know more.

Roger Stevens

A Kiss in Class

I kissed a girl in class today
and, wow, was she surprised.
Her mouth turned even rounder than
the marbles in her eyes.

I thought her cheek would like my kiss,
but that was not the case.
A perfect pink, then purple pool
began to fill her face.

I learned a painful lesson,
and you had better know it.
If you love your teacher,
find another way to show it.

Ted Scheu

Moon at Noon

Mr Warren
Wore a sporran
On St Andrew's Day

But when a gust
His kilt upthrust
Girls screamed and ran away.

Karen Costello-McFeat

What a Rasper

Mr Moses makes us laugh,
Cos everywhere he goes
He lets the biggest rasper out
And thinks nobody knows.

But we've all been behind him
And we've heard him let one rip –
Loud enough to wake the dead
Or sink a cargo ship.

It really is a rasper,
A record-breaking trump,
A real gold-medal winner
Coming out his rump.

And he just keeps on walking
Pretending nothing's wrong,
And they're not only long and loud –
They also leave a pong!

But we've all found the answer
To dear old Mr Moses –
Cotton wool stuffed in our ears
And clothes pegs on our noses . . .

Clive Webster

How to Embarrass Your Headmaster in Assembly

When your headmaster is in assembly
telling his dramatic stories,
pacing up and down and waving his arms . . .

It's always worth waiting until he's halfway through
a really exciting bit before putting your hand up
and loudly saying . . .

Si–ir, why is your zip undone?
And why have you got purple underpants?
And will your trousers fall down, Sir?

He knows they won't fall down
and he knows he hasn't got purple underpants (they're
    red)
but he's not sure whether his zip is undone or not . . .

So, in a flash, he goes bright red,
his hands shoot down in front of his trousers
and he turns round to check . . .

In front of two hundred and fifty laughing children,
the zip is fine and the underpants are not in view
but it is too late, the damage has been done . . .

Mission accomplished,
headmaster embarrassed.
Although this only works if you are Nursery or Year One
    and cute.

Paul Cookson

The Rugby Teacher's Holiday

His muscles bulge inside his shirt,
He charges through the mud and dirt,
Ignoring gale and hail and hurt.

He's more a giant than a man,
He drives a roaring rusty van,
He wears tattoos beneath his tan

And scars across his broken nose
And massive boots with metal toes –
It's just as well that no one knows

When August comes with summer showers
He takes a break from super-powers
And sits indoors and presses flowers.

Clare Bevan

!~#%€* #%**€

Sir said
we shouldn't swear,
'Shows your vocabulary
is very poor.'

Well, our
vocabulary's increased –
he shut his fingers
in the door.

Mike Johnson

Middle Names

Do you know your teacher's middle name?

Maybe it's something potty like Dotty
or silly like Chantilly,
something divine like Columbine
or medicinal like Calomine,
something modern like Ikea
or historical like Boadicea.

Perhaps it's something seasonal
like Primrose,
or a name that gets up your nose
like Hyacinth.

Maybe it's American like Hank
or solid and British like Frank.
Maybe it's barbaric like Conan
or boy-bandish and poppy
like Ronan.

Perhaps it's old-fashioned
like Dora and Norah,
or something buttery
like Flora.

Maybe it's expensive like Pearl
or with a country twang like Merle.
Is it something classy like Clancy
or fancy like Nancy,
something biblical like Zachariah,
Amos, Moses or Jeremiah?

Is it witchy like Winnie
or moany like Minnie,
sensible like Fred,
countrified like Ned?

Is it tragic like Romeo
or Italian like Antonio?

Is it Zebedee or Gertrude,
Marvin or Ermintrude?
Is it Cecil or Boris,
Marmaduke or Doris?

Now go spread rumours
all around school.
Your teachers have names
that just aren't cool.

It's sure to embarrass them!

Brian Moses

The PE Teacher Wants to Be Tarzan

The PE teacher sits and dreams
Of swinging through the trees,
Of taking jungle holidays
And crushing pythons with his knees.

Or running off with nice Miss Jones,
The new biology teacher.
Of taking her to a posh tree house
Where no one else can reach her.

Instead he puffs and pants all day
In a drab and dreary gym
And wishes that there were a spell
For liberating him.

Brian Patten

A Minor Inconvenience

Poor Mrs Ives
rushed off to the loo
although we had heaps
of sums left to do.

When she came back
there were some snickers:
she had her skirt
caught up in her knickers.

Jill Townsend

Mum Goes to Weight Watchers with Mrs Donohue

My mum goes to Weight Watchers with Mrs Donohue
Miss would be embarrassed if she knew the things I knew
What she eats and how last week she gained a pound or
    two
Gossip from the staffroom, who cannot stand who
The teachers and the rumours – some of them are true
My mum goes to Weight Watchers with Mrs Donohue

My mum goes to Weight Watchers with Mrs Donohue
They chit and chat of this and that and what they like to
    do
Mum says Miss can swear and curse so much the air
    turns blue
How she rowed at home, hit her husband with a shoe
The red wine that he spilt on her dress that was brand
    new
My mum goes to Weight Watchers with Mrs Donohue

Then there was the time in aerobic exercise
When she tried to bend too quick and to her surprise
Falling down she slipped and tripped
Her leotard, it stretched and ripped
Bursting open to reveal her knickers, old and blue
All these secrets I have kept
I've not told anybody . . . yet
My mum goes to Weight Watchers with Mrs Donohue

Paul Cookson

Mr Jones's Rock-and-Roll Dream

The other day I came across something quite grotesque
It was Mr Jones, our teacher, standing on his desk
He was strumming on a ruler with his right hand
Just like a guitarist in a rock-and-roll band
He waggled his hips
Pursed his lips
And then began to wail,
'I'm the baddest teacher and I oughta be in jail!'

Then he turned and saw me smiling by the door.
He'll never play at pop stars at school any more.

John Coldwell

Hair Today, Gone Tomorrow

There was a teacher at my school
Who always picked on me
This teacher's name was Mr Twigg
And he taught us PE.

Now Mr Twigg kept a secret
That he dared not give away
But more through luck than judgement
I found it out one day.

Spying through the staffroom keyhole
Is, I know, a childish jape
But I found out Twiggy's secret
Involved strips of sticky tape.

Thinking how to use this secret
A cunning plan I then did hatch
That involved the long-awaited
Staff v Pupils rugby match.

Now rugby is a game I liked
I played it rather well
But whether my great plan would work
Only time would tell.

When the match day came, I felt
Excitement tinged with fear
A massive crowd turned out to watch
The grudge match of the year.

I kicked the ball to Mr Twigg
Who caught it well and ran
But I lined him up and tackled him
Then carried out my plan.

As we lay there in the mud
I reached towards his head
But left the ball which was close by
And grabbed his hair instead.

As players from both sides approached us
Looking to secure the ball
I pulled hard on Twiggy's hairpiece
And it came off, tape and all.

Climbing to his feet, embarrassed
Both his hands went to his head
Then in words I cannot mention
He shouted that I'd soon be dead.

As I ran a lap of honour
Holding up his secret wig
At long last I'd got my own back
On that nasty Mr Twigg.

Richard Caley

Tricks with my new rubber mouse

It's got long wobbly whiskers
and a realistic squeak
so I took it to school
been dying to all week.

I thought I'd trick our teacher
dear trembly Mr Taut
he's such a jumpy, twitchy chap
a very nervous sort.

We were doing numeracy
decimals and fractions
but I had pre-arranged
several small distractions.

First Luke gave Jack a shove
said he'd pinched his pen
so Jack shoved Luke back in the front
and Luke shoved Jack again.

Emma's nose began to bleed
Ryan had a faint
then Sarah started being sick
in the powder paint.

Poor Mr Taut was very fraught
rushing here and there
he didn't notice that I'd popped
my mouse beneath his chair.

It all calmed down eventually
he sat down on his seat
then he turned pale when he saw
my mouse crouched at his feet.

'OH YUCK,' he yelled jumping up
and racing through the door.
'A MOUSE, A MOUSE, I'VE NEVER SEEN
ONE SO HUGE BEFORE.'

Our laughter ended when a voice
boomed, 'ENOUGH OF THAT!'
It was Jonesy our head teacher
with a rounders bat.

He strode across towards my mouse
and gave it such a thump
it didn't squash, it didn't squeal
just gave a little jump.

Mr Taut said, trembling,
'Please tell me that it's dead.'
'It isn't real,' said Mr Jones
and slowly shook his head.

'It's just a toy, you silly man,'
continued Mr Jones.
'No squeak, no skin, no nasty bite
no teeth, no eyes, no bones.'

'I'm afraid that you've been fooled
by your class, however
you really must stop blubbing, man
pull yourself together.'

Well Jonesy thinks he's really tough
I'll get him too, make no mistake
tomorrow in assembly
I'm bringing my pet snake.

David Harmer

Skimpily Red

I've never seen Miss Nixon
so flustered or so vexed
as when I saw her picking up
a pair of pants in Next.

Miss Nixon's rather strict and prim.
She teaches us RE.
The knickers she was purchasing
were silk and r-e-d.

I grinned at her. She put them back,
looked guilty as a thief.
I couldn't help but notice
they were very, very brief.

Her eyes met mine. She gave me such
a long hard icy stare,
and said, 'Will Johnson! Why are you
in Ladies' Underwear?'

As scarlet as those skimpy pants
I felt my face glow red.
Then mum looked up, peered round the stand.
'My son's with me,' she said.

Celia Gentles

Spelling Test

If you hate spelling as much as me,
There's something you should do.
Just give your teacher a spelling test
That's worse than she gives you.

Say, 'Miss, could you help me spell the word
Onomatopoeia*?'
Then add, 'I'm having trouble again,
Now with logorrhoea*.'

Onomatopoeia:
O-N-N-E-R ... no ...
O-N-A-M ... er ...
H-O-N-O-U-R ...
Oh! B-U-M!

Then, when she's fading and wishing for
Literacy hour to end,
Try inaugurate* and zucchini*
To drive her round the bend.

After that, if you get zero
On your next spelling test,
You can say, 'I'm sure *you* understand.
I really did my best!'

Karen Costello-McFeat

Impress your friends with these words too:
Onomatopoeia refers to sound words like *bang!*
Logorrhoea is talking too much
Inaugurate is to begin a job with a ceremony
Zucchini is another word for courgette

Mr Roberts

Mr Roberts
   (morning prayers)
fell asleep
   (on teachers' chairs).
We all marched out
and went to classes
leaving him with snores
and glasses.
Come PE –
   (in the hall)
Mr Roberts missed it all
then quickly stood
   (at half past ten)
and shouted out
   a loud
      AMEN.

Peter Dixon

Nothing Doing

Mr Newton blew a gasket –
  he just flew into a rage
when the homework that I passed him
  had no words upon the page.

'If I had a million dollars . . .'
  Mr Newton had us write,
which is why I handed over
  just the blankest sheet of white.

'You've done nothing!' teacher hollered.
  'Yes,' I told him, 'that is true –
if I had a million dollars,
  that's *precisely* what I'd do!'

Graham Denton

School Camp Photo Project

We had to do a project on our school camp trip away
Evidence and photographs for a class display

I worked really hard, did ever such a lot
Can't wait to put it on the wall and see what I have got

Dozing on the coach – there's Mr Flynn
Mouth wide open, dribble on his chin

That one's Mr Cox – finger up his nose
Didn't think anyone was looking, I suppose

This one's Mrs Rose – first thing in the morning
It should have a Government Health Warning!

Now here's our head teacher – this one's really good
It's when he slipped and went full length in the mud

Look at Mr Watson posing by the pool
His trunks are falling down, but he thinks he's looking
   cool

Trendy in her swimsuit, sweet and young Miss Cotton
Everybody noticed the tattoo on her . . .

Last thing at night, that's Mr Chalmers
In his rabbit slippers and his pink silk pyjamas

Everyone loved it, we all had a laugh
All my friends want copies of my photographs

But the staff did not laugh at the pictures that they saw
Now I'm sitting . . . waiting . . . worried . . . by the head
   teacher's door!

Paul Cookson

Bottom of the Class

He scribbles on the blackboard.
We giggle and we laugh.
He thinks the joke he told is good.
He doesn't know the half!
For our joke is better –
we chalked a yellow 'V'
upon his chair and now it's on
his trousers, for all to see.

Gina Douthwaite

Summer Fête Fun

Our head teacher's in the stocks
he's pretending that it's fun
and for five minutes at least
there's nowhere he can run!

Which is why we're going to give
everything we've got,
wet sponges, buckets, hosepipes –
he can have the lot!

The only problem is
our teachers have got there first,
there's no stopping them
they're out to do their worst!

It doesn't seem quite fair
as we watch him getting wet
but at least it'll be a lesson
our head teacher won't forget.

Andrew Collett

Did Miss Enjoy the Movie?

I saw Miss Smith at the pictures
I sat down right behind her
She didn't know that I was there
But often I remind her.

She sat there with her boyfriend
A friendly-looking chap
Sharing popcorn from a tub
Which nestled in her lap.

He put his arm around her
He stroked her soft brown hair
But when he turned and kissed her
I sat rooted to my chair.

This was great, two things to watch
The film and Miss Smith too
Perhaps I should have turned away
But then again, would you?

At the end the credits rolled
And what came next was groovy
As they rose to leave I said
'Did Miss enjoy the movie?'

I saw Miss Smith at the pictures
I sat down right behind her
She didn't know that I was there
But often I remind her.

Richard Caley

Mr Higson's Lament

Mr Higson, you're our favourite
Teacher in the school
And we know sandals aren't trendy
And we know tank tops aren't cool

And you've patches on your elbows
And your jacket's second best
And the waistband on your trousers
Comes up to your chest

But we don't mind that, Mr Higson
How you dress is up to you
But there's only one thing that we ask
One thing we wish you'd do

Glue your wig on, Mr Higson
Cos it keeps on falling off
It wriggles and it jiggles
Every time you cough

It's distracting in assembly
And in maths it puts us off
Glue your wig on, Mr Higson
Cos it keeps on falling off

In football when you refereed
And I was Ashley Cole
Your wig blew off, I missed the ball
And your wig scored the goal

A bald head's not so bad, you know
That's why we're telling you
Release your wig into the wild
Or buy a pot of glue

Roger Stevens

'I Want a Word with You Lot . . .'

'I want a word with you lot,'
The new teacher said.
Out came the butter,
The knife and the bread.
'We hope the word's tasty,'
The cheeky class said.
'We hope it's not SPROUT,
Or CABBAGE or FISH
(Or anything healthy poured into a dish).
A good word would be
SAUSAGE or CHOCOLATE or PIE,
And CAKE is a word
For which we'd all die.'

'Enough of this nonsense!
I'm fed up, I'm through!
You'll all eat your words
When I'm finished with you.
The word I want
Is not one word, but two
That when stuck together
Make you feel blue.
You all know it well,
You loathe it, you shirk
From facing up to
That word
　　　　　HOMEWORK.'

Brian Patten

Watch It, Miss, Or Else!

Don't tell me off for shouting, Miss,
Or I'll be forced to say
What I heard you call the referee
At the match on Saturday.

Don't give me extra homework, Miss,
Don't you ever, ever dare
Or else I'll have to tell the class
About the wig you wear.

Don't keep me in at playtime, Miss,
Cos I couldn't do that sum
Or else I'll have to tell the head
That you were chewing gum.

Don't make me do my spellings again
Or I will have, I fear,
To tell the inspector how you spelt
'Disapoint' and 'disapear'.

Don't tell me off for running, Miss,
Or I'll say that I saw
Your knickers when you turned cartwheels
Across the classroom floor.

Don't ever pick on me again
Or else I'll have to tell
I saw you kissing Mr West
Down by the wishing well!

John Foster

A Spell to Make the Headmaster's Trousers Fall Down During Assembly

When nobody can see you
Run backwards round the hall
Do this six times and six times more
To see those trousers fall
Spit upon your fingers
Rub them on your nose
Stick your left thumb in your right ear
Wiggle all your toes
Take ten rubber bands
And seven lengths of string
When the hall begins to fill
Softly start to sing.

Oh Headmaster, oh Headmaster
Your slacks are getting slacker
When this spell starts working
It will be a cracker
Your elasticated waistband
Will start to lose its grip
Your knobbly knees will feel the breeze
When those trousers slip.

Begin to cut the string
And snap the rubber bands
Cross your eyes, hold your breath
Clap with both your hands
Jump up and down, spin round and round
Shout 'Trousers, drop down quick'
Then the teachers and the children
Will see your magic trick.
His trousers round his ankles
His spotty pants on view
Your poor red-faced headmaster
Just won't know what to do.

David Harmer

It Won't Be All Right on the Night!

Welcome to tonight's show
And in our first clip
Here's Miss Brown at break time looking for the board
    rubber.
But what does she do when she can't find it?
Takes off her shoe, spits on her sock and uses that
    instead.
Didn't see those Y5s watching through the window
With the camera phone, did you, Miss?

Next up
It's Mr Smith in the science lesson
Painting his nails pink to teach Y6
All about varnish hardening and going off.
But oh dear, someone's hidden the nail-polish remover.
The only thing that's hardening and going off now is Mr
    Smith's smile,
As his nails stay Barbie pink all day.
Thanks to the Y3 team making the school documentary
    for that one.

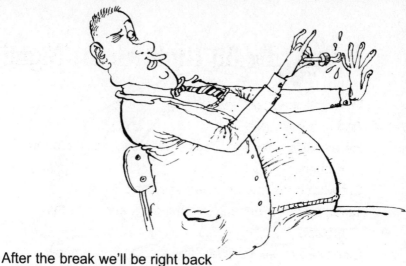

After the break we'll be right back
With Mr Jones the geography teacher
And that moment captured on video
When he got Y4 lost on the map-reading trip.
Don't go away!

Welcome back,
And in our viewers' favourites section this week,
Back by popular demand,
Here's that moment on residential when Mrs Large
    capsized the dinghy,
Then Ms Green with the toilet door handle coming off in
    her hand,
And yes, that maths test with Mr Black walking up and
    down in squeaky new shoes,
Turning smartly
And falling over a strategically placed bag.

Well, that's nearly all we've got time for
But last up before we go
It's Mr Small and his funny tummy.
That tummy's been gurgling and groaning all morning,
But now there's dead silence in the English exam when
    he stands up to announce:
'You've got five minutes to go,'
Sits down
And breaks wind loudly.

Goodnight!

Michael Lockwood

Double Fault

Poor Mrs Johnson's in terrible pain,
she just had to take the day off once again;
incredibly, when I watched *Tennis Report*,
there was her double, front row, Centre Court.

Mike Johnson

Head Teacher

Mr Dawkins liked to shout
until the day his teeth shot out.
Across the hall his false teeth flew
and landed in a pot of glue!
He's still our head,
he comes each day
but never has a lot to say.

Peter Dixon

Miss Fidgetbum

There's a teacher in our school
We call Miss Fidgetbum
She says she teaches numeracy
But we just call it sums.

Takes her glasses on and off . . .
She'll scratch, she'll sniff, she'll sniff again
She'll go harrumph and cough.

We play a game around our group:
Pass a coin from hand to hand.
It stops each time she sniffs or coughs
And we all understand

That if you've got it in your fist
You must remove a shoe
And it goes on and on like this
With socks also removed . . .

First one to have both feet quite bare
Is the loser in the game
But it makes the lesson much more fun
So it isn't such a shame.

We concentrate on all she does;
We never talk or laugh;
Miss Fidgetbum thinks we're really good
– she doesn't know the half!

Trevor Millum

Oh Mr Porter!

When he takes us swimming at Mornington Baths
Our teacher Mr Porter
Wears fancy swimwear in designer pink
But he never goes near the water.

He has carefully combed hair and muscles to spare
Has our debonair Mr Porter
And a badge to show the medals he's won
Though he's never been seen in the water.

He strides up and down with his megaphone
Does the elegant Mr Porter
And expertly shows us the various strokes
But his toe never touches the water.

It's rumoured he swam for England one time
It's a rumour he won't deny
And it's said he took bronze in the freestyle race
And struck gold in the butterfly.

We went this year to Rocca del Mar
For a holiday by the sea
And as we played on the beach one day
Who should I chance to see

But the suntanned figure in designer shades
Of the muscular Mr Porter
And unobserved I watched as he jogged
Down to the sparkling water.

He smiled at the girls as he combed his hair
Then he lay in the waves like a log
Before flopping on to his sunburned front
And paddling like a dog.

And then Mr Porter, you dog-paddling fraud
You caught sight of me looking at you
And in that instant you understood
That I knew that you knew that I knew.

Gareth Owen

I Can't Believe It

You won't believe it
I don't believe it
It's grotesque!
What our teacher gets up to
Every weekend.

It's not that she's fat
It's not that she's hairy
But she's nearly twenty-seven
And that's so old it's scary!

Zak says his mum told him
Because she knows her
And Zak swears it's true.

Teacher's a naturist.
Zak's mum said it's not rude.
Every weekend
She takes off all her clothes
And runs around
In the nude!

Roger Stevens

Caught

We saw you Miss in the supermarket
Filling your trolley
With
Bottles of pop
Boxes of sweets
Burgers and chocolate
And other sticky treats.

And what do you tell us this week
Should be in our diet?
Cabbage!
If it's that great
Then why don't you try it?

John Coldwell

The Day Our Teacher Fell Off His Chair

How I wish that you'd been there
The day our teacher fell off his chair.
Seat on the floor, feet in the air
The day our teacher fell off his chair.

Very far from debonair
Growling like a grizzly bear
Used rude words, began to swear
The day our teacher fell off his chair.

Beware! Beware! Laugh if you dare!
He yelled at us, we didn't care
We saw red-spotted underwear
The day our teacher fell off his chair.

A punctured beach ball losing air
Blocking off the thoroughfare
Between the whiteboard's blank-faced stare
And his creaky, cranky chair.

How our laughter filled the air
The day our teacher fell off his chair!

David Harmer

All Creatures Great and Small

All things bright and beautiful
All creatures great and small
All things live and wonderful
Our teacher hates them all

The spider in her teacup
The wasp inside her socks
The cockroach in the sandwich
The ants in her lunch box

The skunk stuck in the storeroom
The mouse inside her desk
The beetles in her trainers
Climbing up her dress

The caterpillars creeping
On to her new permed hair
The stick insects all sticking
In her underwear

The bumblebees that hide in
The pockets of her coat
The frogs inside her handbag
The lizard round her throat

All things bright and beautiful
All creatures great and small
We bring them and our teacher's
Embarrassed by them all.

The noises that she screams out
The way she jumps up high
The way she runs round the room
The fear in her eyes

Like a cartoon human
She entertains the masses
She is wild and wonderful
Embarrassed in her classes

Paul Cookson

How to Embarrass Your Teacher

1. If you see your teacher slip on a banana skin, do you:
   a) Help them to their feet and get them a soothing cup of coffee?
   b) Pretend you didn't see?
   c) Throw another three banana skins, plus a tub of jelly and a vat of grease and watch the rest of the staff fall over as well?

2. If Miss Happ comes out of the ladies' staff loo with her dress accidentally tucked into her underwear, do you:
   a) Find an appropriate moment to let her know so she can rearrange herself in private?
   b) Wish you hadn't seen?
   c) Shout out at the top of your voice, 'Oi, Miss! I didn't realize giant purple-spotted bloomers were back in fashion!'?

3. *You hear your teacher burp very loudly. Do you:*
   a) Say, 'Pardon me, Sir,' and give him some indigestion tablets as you take the blame?
   b) Roll your eyes in disgust?
   c) Shout, 'Good one, Sir! Is there shipping in this area?'

4. *Your teacher bends over to pick up a pencil. When she isn't looking, do you:*
   a) Pick it up for her?
   b) Look the other way and get on with your work?
   c) Place a large drawing pin upright on the chair she is about to sit on?

5. *Your teacher accidentally leave his briefcase unattended. Do you:*
   a) Close it for him?
   b) Carry on chattering to your mate?
   c) Load it with last week's sandwiches, some frogspawn, dandruff from Eddie's head and a pair of sweaty football socks?

6. You notice your teacher nodding off during the head teacher's particularly boring assembly. Do you:

    a) Gently nudge her awake?

    b) Try not to nod off yourself?

    c) Don't tell her when assembly has finished and leave her alone, telling everyone else to leave the hall on tiptoe?

7. Fat Bob, the greedy Year 6 teacher, has spilt half a plate of mushy peas down his tie. Do you:

    a) Hand him a tissue?

    b) Try hard not to look at the sickening sight?

    c) Shout, 'Are you saving those peas for later, Sir, or have you sneezed?'

8. On concert night, your teacher is playing the piano. Do you:

    a) Politely applaud every note?

    b) Stay at home and watch the telly?

    c) Offer to turn the music over and drop the lid on her fingers at any given moment?

9. On open night, your teacher discusses 'little Janet's' spelling with your parents. Do you:

    a) Apologize and correct all the mistakes?

    b) Turn up your iPod?

    c) Point out that actually you are called Liam?

10. You notice during assembly that the headmaster's wig is in danger of being dislodged thanks to the breeze from the open window. Do you:

  a) Close the window immediately?
  b) Go back to sleep?
  c) Get all your mates to count to three and blow really hard?

If you mainly scored a:
You are the teacher's pet and an utterly weedy creep.

If you mainly scored b:
You really couldn't care less, could you? Hey, WAKE UP!! I'M TALKING TO YOU!!

If you mainly scored c:
You are a very successful embarrassment to your teacher. Well done!

David Harmer and Paul Cookson